A POETIC HISTORY OF MELBOURNE

A POETIC HISTORY OF MELBOURNE

An anthology of poems and short stories by students

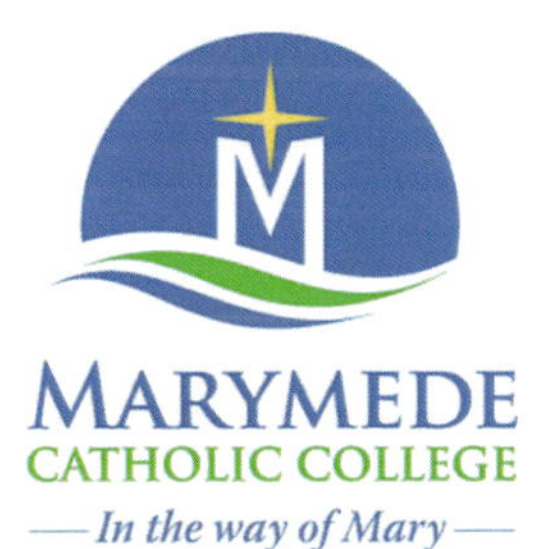

Editor: John Milides

ARCADIA

© The authors of *A Poetic History of Melbourne*

Published in 2022 by ARCADIA
the international general books' imprint of
Australian Scholarly Publishing Pty Ltd

Australian Scholarly Publishing Ltd
7 Lt Lothian St Nth, North Melbourne, VIC 3051
Tel: 03 9329 6963 / Fax: 03 9329 5452
enquire@scholarly.info / www.scholarly.info

in association with Marymede Catholic College
60 Williamsons Road
South Morang, Victoria 3752
Australia

Tel: 03 9407 9000
http://www.marymede.vic.edu.au

ISBN 978-0-646-85154-9

Acknowledgment of the photographs and historical information in this book:

We acknowledge and we thank the Australian War Memorial, the State Library of Victoria, Museums Victoria, the National Museum of Australia, the National Library of Australia, for the photographs and histories of Melbourne and Victoria, posted in their respective websites. We also acknowledge the facebook site Melbourne & Victoria – Through the Decades, and Mr Dennis Noone, and all the people posting royalty-free photos on this site.

Cover photograph: Flinders Street Railway Station, 1927. It opened in 1854 to serve the metropolitan rail network and some country services.

Contents

Introduction

A Poetic History of Melbourne

The Creative Writing Program is an extra-curriculum program running after school every week. It is open for all students in the secondary school. Students learn the art of writing poetry and short stories. Our goal was to write a history of Melbourne through poetry. In 2019, the enthusiastic students who participated were: Larissa Blazevski (Year 7), James Champlin (Year 8), Cecilia Bingham (Year 9), Antonio Bentovski (Year 9), Shanti Pisani (year 9) and Chloe Falzon (year 11).

We studied the important milestones in the history of Melbourne and the students wrote poems exploring the importance of moments and people in its history. Although Melbourne is one of the youngest cities in the world, (it was established in 1835), students learnt that Melbourne has given the world a lot of firsts. For example, Melbourne is the first city in the world to pass legislation to offer free education to all students! It is the first city in the world where working people fought and won the 8-hour working day! We started studying the history of Melbourne in 2019 and at the same time writing poetry about significant moments in Melbourne's history. We were planning to continue in 2020 but unfortunately, we were hit by the coronavirus pandemic. The whole world almost went into lockdown including of course us, in Melbourne. We spent nearly the whole year of 2020 in lockdown, and we were learning remotely. It was therefore impossible to work on our goal, as we could not get together as a group. In 2021, new students joined the program Janelle Kauseni (Year 7), Divinia Kihara (Year 7), Sandra Panamthathu (Year 7), Casey Ennis (Year 8), Emily Tricarico (Year 9), and therefore they gave life and hope to our goal.

However, more lockdowns ensued in 2021, more remote learning, less days when we could meet as a group. It became very difficult to continue teaching the program to write our history of Melbourne in poetry. Thanks to my students' dedication, we continued against all odds, and we started again classes after school, whenever it was possible, under very difficult circumstances. As a result, we managed to achieve our goal by the end of 2021!

I would like to thank all my students for keeping up with the pace of the program under extremely difficult circumstances for learning and for writing, especially poetry, as we tried to imagine how it would have been like for the first pioneers of Melbourne, for the Wurundjeri indigenous Australians of Melbourne who came into contact for the first time with the first white settlers, for the stonemasons who downed their tools in order to win the 8 hour working day for the working people of the whole world (!), for the miners of the Eureka Stockage, for the ANZAC soldiers who decided to offer their service and risk their lives to go and fight to defend Europe, for the Olympic champion athletes of the 1956 Olympic Games, the migrants who came to Melbourne after the Second World War, to an unknown land, a different language and a new culture.

We hope that the reader of this book would appreciate our attempt which we think is an original attempt to write the history of Melbourne in poetry. We hope that we have done justice to the city of Melbourne, the people of Melbourne, the people whose histories we tried to give voice to, and we hope that other students and other schools would follow our example to dedicate some time to study the histories of their communities and to give voice to the unsung heroes of their communities. We hope that our poetry and short stories would liberate the mind of the reader and give more meaning to our coexistence and cohabitation in this beautiful place that we call Melbourne!

John Milides, Teacher of the Creative Writing Program
B.A. (Hons)
Dipl. of Education
Post-Grad. Dipl. Educational Studies
Master of Education

Prologue by Marymede College Principals

I found it fascinating to take a step back in time to relive the impact of the first Europeans arriving in Melbourne in 1835 and how it changed the lives of the Aborigines living in the area.

The impact of the Gold Rush in Ballarat in 1951 resulted in boatloads of people travelling from overseas in search of their fortune. The Eureka Stockade; the introduction of the 8-hour working day; the first free compulsory and secular education; the birth of Aussie Rules Football and its impact on the community and the 1956 Melbourne Olympic Games were other highlights for me.

I was saddened to read about the treatment of the ANZACs who were taken prisoner and I hope that our students never forget why ANZAC Day is such an important day in our country's rich history.

The reference at the end to how the students would like to see Melbourne in the future was a great way to finish what was a very powerful book.

I congratulate the students and their teacher Mr John Milides for their perseverance as they were forced to work from home for the majority of the past two years. They rarely had the chance to meet face to face and were having to deal with their own issues in lockdown. They can feel proud of what they have achieved.

I hope this book inspires other students to take up the art of writing poetry and short stories.

Michael Kenny, Principal of Marymede Catholic College 2015 — 21

Congratulations to the students of Marymede Catholic College who have contributed their writing to *A Poetic History of Melbourne*. The poetry and short stories offer a wonderful range of reflections on the history of Melbourne. Students have worked hard with the support of their Teacher, Mr John Milides, to produce poetry and short stories of a very high standard. The insights into various elements of Melbourne's history share stories that not everyone will be aware of. Melbourne has a rich history to be proud of and to learn from. I hope that readers of this literature learn about Melbourne and may consider reading further and even writing their own poems and short stories about Melbourne. Congratulations again to John Milides and the students on this excellent collection of writing!

Timothy Newcomb, Principal, 2022

1835
The beginning of Melbourne

The first owners of the land

The Boon Wurrung and Woi Wurrung (Wurundjeri) peoples of the Kulin Nation were the first inhabitants of the area where the modern city of Melbourne was established in 1835.

"The arrival of Europeans in Victoria irrevocably changed the lives of the many Aboriginal groups inhabiting the area. Initial conciliation gave way to European arrogance and Aboriginal resentment stemming from the settlers' exclusive idea of property.

Following John Batman's "purchase" of a portion of Aboriginal land the arrival of the pastoralists spelled the end of Aborigines' traditional way of life. Whilst various tribes resisted the takeover of

Aboriginal group of men and women, 1871, photographer unknown

their lands, they were no match for the well-armed and determined Europeans and the inevitable result was loss of life and dislocation.

The system of Aboriginal protectorates introduced in 1836, and presided over by George Augustus Robinson from 1839, collapsed under the pressure of the settlers' land hunger and was scrapped within a decade. Reserves also failed, and whilst the missions provided a refuge for many people it was necessary for them to conform to strict rules which undermined their traditional way of life."

State Library of Victoria

Inscribed in Robert Russell's hand:
Collins Street Melbourne Looking West 1838.

View along Collins Street looking west towards Market Street, from approximately Russell Street. Several sailing ships can be seen in the Pool to the left of Collins Street and a group of Aboriginal people are surveying the scene from the high ground in the foreground of the image. A vegetable garden surrounded by a picket fence can be seen lower right.

Robert Russell was born near London in 1808; surveyor, architect, and artist; on 10th September 1836 Russell was appointed surveyor to the infant settlement at Port Phillip and he arrived in the area on 5th October 1836; Robert Hoddle superseded him in 1837.

Imagining the Dreamtime birth[1]

I lay in the endlessly silent void,
uncoiling from my place of rest.
Trapped under layers of mantle and crust, I rise.
My stomach heavy,
my limbs long as I wind a path through the earth.
Calling out to the creatures in hiding,
laughing as a liquid life rushes through my pathways.
Animals rush out as crashing ensues,
water seeping effortlessly into the soil.
Tall figures emerge from the ground
their arms swaying in the breeze, whistling, and calling out to me.
The barren land I rested under, now full of life,
of creatures large and small,
their movements sculpting each rough surface,
exploring each cloud.
For those who listen, I grant them a new form,
a human form,
a totem remains the only reminder of a past.
Merging, mingling, they learn the language of my earth,
singing for their brothers and sisters,
mothers and fathers,

---

1 Imagining the Dreamtime birth: a poem dedicated to the Dreamtime of the First Nation Peoples of Australia

their homes.
They carve hollow cylinders from eucalyptus trees,
their sound carries from tribe to tribe,
growing with time.
Sharing songs,
their paintings populate my creation,
their steps are passed down from generation to generation.
My story is told.

Emily Tricarico

The fruit of a city[2]

It all started with a seed,
a small seed of hopes and dreams,
that grew slowly but surely,
sprouting into the place, we call home.
Each passing day the seed grew,
its vines twisting and turning into the future,
the warm, burning sun shone down onto its leaves,
the rough, dry earth blanketing its roots,
it held its head high to the bright blue abyss.
Over the years it towered over the surrounding planes
it had its faults,
wilting, shrivelling when the heat becomes too much
but now our seed is a tree standing strong,
large, thick, covered in a variety of fruits,
all have come from around the world,
the fruit of a city,
our city,
Melbourne.

Cecilia Bingham

---

2 Naming Melbourne — In 1837 a small settlement on the banks of the Yarra River in Australia needed a name. Queen Victoria, after whom the State of Victoria is named, decided that it would be named Melbourne. This was as an honour for the 2nd Viscount Melbourne, British Prime Minister, and the political mentor to the young Queen.

John Batman speaks, 1835

Adepiction of Batman's meeting with the Wurundjeri Aborigines at Merri Creek and the alleged signing of Batman's 'treaty'. John Wesley Burtt, circa 1875. Painting: oil on canvas.

"When John Batman arrived in Port Phillip in 1836, he approached local Indigenous leaders with a contract, to 'buy' their land. He claimed his negotiations were successful, and as a result he owned 240,000 hectares of prime farming terrain – almost all of the Kulin people's ancestral land.

This painting also shows laid out on blankets some of the items Batman offered the Wurundjeri in return for their lands, including mirrors, shirts and beads — a token payment for an enormous stretch of valuable land.

Like many depictions of this event, it was created more than forty years after the events shown. It is also interesting to note there are no images of Batman that were created while he was alive, so we don't know what he actually looked like.

Batman's treaty was almost immediately declared invalid by the Proclamation of Governor Bourke of New South Wales. On 6 August 1835, he declared the British Crown owned the entire land of Australia, and that only it could sell or distribute land."

State Library of Victoria

"Simon Wonga was a Wurundjeri elder who was one of the first Aboriginal leaders to successfully regain lands taken by settlers and he also secured land that later become the Coranderrk Aboriginal mission, where he died in about 1875." The Age, Feb. 16, 2017

John Batman,
the founder of Melbourne

John Batman, born in Rosehill
in eighteen hundred and one
desired a status of more than just a convict's son.

A farmer in Van Diemen's Land.
An explorer and pioneer at heart,
an expedition to the mainland
brought his new life to a start.

In 1835 his venture began
to establish a new settlement in a new land,
the natives' land, in exchange for goods:
Flour, knives, blankets, and clothing to wear.

A signed deed with the Aboriginals
to work, to build and share,
for this was a place for a village
John Batman's proposal seemed fair.

The New South Wales government,
claimed his treaty an invalid offer,
but with growth in the community
the land continued to prosper.

People kept coming, a new city was born.
Batman, the founder of Batmania.
Later called Melbourne for all,
the most beautiful city in Australia.

Larissa Blazevski

John Batman speaks

A land of opportunity.
I have gifted blankets,
axes,
flour,
and other goods.
In return,
I have received a legacy.

Chloe Falzon

July 6, 1835
Melbourne must not forget
William Buckley

"The first settlers discover Buckley", Frederick William Woodhouse (1820-1909)

"William Buckley was born in Macclesfield, England, in 1780. As a young man he worked briefly as an apprentice bricklayer, but soon joined the army and became a respected soldier. He served for four years in the King's own Regiment of Foot and embarked under the Duke of York for Holland. He was there wounded in an engagement and returned to England. However, his military career came to an abrupt end in 1802, when he was accused of theft and sentenced to 14 years in the convict colony of Australia.

In October 1803, Buckley arrived at the convict settlement at Sullivan Bay, on the Calcutta. However, a lack of fresh water and difficult conditions made the settlement less than satisfactory, and many convicts attempted escape. Buckley was one of the few that succeeded.

On Christmas Eve 1803 he escaped, until he reached the area near Barwon Heads, where he lived with the Wathaurung Indigenous people for the next 32 years. Over this time, he was accepted into the Aboriginal community and culture, and made a crucial first step towards understanding between white settlers and the Indigenous people.

On the 6th of July 1835, he walked into John Batman's camp. Buckley became an important translator in negotiations with the local Indigenous tribesmen."

State Library of Victoria

Melbourne should remember William Buckley

A rage of water lashed at my face,
it ran down my throat as I took deep breaths
coughing and screaming into the night sky
as I rushed further into the darkness,
the waves hammered in my ears
as I pushed forward into a blind destination,
the midnight heat burning my skin,
my heart is slowing as I sink deeper and deeper
into the waves,
Darkness.
The sand was hot and stuck to my skin.
I lay motionless on the coast,
the waves lash at my face.
I stare into the endless void
laying outstretched exhausted on shoreline.
It was peaceful,
but a calm spot in the middle of hell.
My hands clutched the wet sand
leaving a cave of dirt below it.
The air was thick and warm.
It sank into my lungs as the feelings started to set,
trapped yet free,

worse than dead,
far away from home.
I sat up,
groaning while doing so,
the will to survive slowly
slipping through my fingers like grains of sand.
I walked along the coast stumbling with each step.
Soon I reunited with a handful of people,
the ones who had joined me in my escape to nowhere.
They were stranded here too,
the ones who were left.
I started to wonder what would have been better,
hell on earth, or here, something much worse.
Days upon days we walked and searched,
there was nothing.
This place was a wasteland.
Some men fell to the heat and exhaustion,
it was painful to leave them behind.
Others turned to leave,
taking many of the other men with them,
at least then, some might have a chance of survival,
the cowards,
I kept on moving,
each coming day
slower and slower,
each coming day,
hotter and hotter,
everything was dry,
everything was dusty.
My body shook with the passing hours,

I grabbed onto whatever I could,
any nutrition I could
my hands clutched onto a spear
that sat alone on the earth,
I hung onto it with all my might,
it may be the key to my survival,
my mind sank deeper into the delusion,
my eyes fell shut despite my body's efforts,
my muscles let go of the hold
darkness,
a tug on my shoulder startled me awake
as a looked up at my presumed attacker.
Yet eyes of kindness looked
upon my shrivelled waste of a body.
A village of aboriginal people stood above me.
Thirty-two years of living and loving
my aboriginal protectors came to an end.
I awoke to see different people.
They were white like me,
but they were strangers.
They offered me bread.
I uttered an English word: "bread"
after thirty-two years of speaking Wathaurung.

As I left, I could hear their cries.
They mourned for me as I was taken away.
Further and further, I realised what I had done,
I had betrayed them
As I made them sign away their life and souls.
I did not belong with the white men.

Now I was surely not wanted with any family,
Aboriginal or white.
I held onto a broken bridge
trying to keep it together,
even though I had torn it apart.
I left Melbourne for ever
To Van Diemen's Land.

Cecilia Bingham

William Buckley's Poem

As a boy I worked with bricks,
assembled layers upon layers of bricks.
It was challenging work, and the pay was poor.
As my parents passed away young,
it was my responsibility to provide for my siblings,
I was the oldest, a young man of twenty-two years.
I worked longer, harder, and still received the same pay.
Despite the poverty we lived in,
the lack of food and water,
we were encompassed with each other's love, warmth,
and comfort.

On a cold and disastrous day, I must say,
after a tiring and restless 10-hour labour,
I received only two six shillings.
This was the third day my earnings were poor.
I couldn't afford to buy a single piece of bread.
My siblings were starving, as was myself.
I had no other choice.
I joined the army, I trained,
sent off to fight in the Netherlands,
to fight Napoleon's troops,
I got shot in the hand,
I was returned to London.

Not a day goes by when I don't regret accepting a roll of cloth.
They claimed I accepted stolen goods!
I said I had no idea!
No mercy for an injured soldier
who fought for King and Country!

My sentence – To be transported to New South Wales
as a convict for fifteen years!
Is this justice?

Here I am, one year later in this unknown land.
I was shipped away from my home, my family.
I never had a chance to say goodbye.
Here, they make us work long hours,
Crashing stones, clearing land, digging.
Along with my other convict mates,
we suffer, we sweat, we slave.
All for a roll of cloth.

Little did I know that Christmas Eve, 1803, would change
my life.
Along with my three mates, we agreed to escape this torture,
this injustice.
That night, as we worked on building the framework for a
store house,
most of the guards were drinking, unaware,
we seized our chance.
We stole a kettle, a gun, boots and medical supplies,
and we ran away leaving the convict settlement,
never looking back.

The guards were chasing after us, commanding us to halt,
we never did.

Charles Shaw, was shot, certainly injured but we had no choice,
we ran towards the bushes and made our escape.
We made slow progress toward Port Phillip Bay,
surviving on shellfish and succulent pants.
We were still lacking proper food, shelter and clean water.
The others feared the Aboriginals,
feared they would kill us for stealing and intruding their land.
They gave up, ran away to Sullivan Bay, or back to the
convict settlement.
I wonder what happened to them, I never saw them again.
I was no coward though, I had nothing to fear.
My family, life and free-will stolen from me.
Desperate, hungry, thirsty and tired,
I had no hope of surviving.
I was all alone.
Or was I?
The aboriginal tribes, I had thought of as savages,
proved to be my saviours.
At last, I found justice with the natives.

Antonio Bentovski

1851
The Victorian Gold Rush

Gold in Victoria

Gold mining, Navarre/Barkly area, 1861.
Daintree, Richard, 1832-1878, photographer

"Towards the end of August 1851, James Reagan and John Dunlop discovered the richest goldfield the world has ever seen in a place the Aborigines called Ballarat, which means 'camping place', now the city of Ballarat. Other discoveries soon followed in Mount Alexander, now called Castlemaine, in Daylesford, Creswick, Maryborough, Bendigo and McIvor, now called Heathcote. Thousands of people left their homes and jobs and set off to the

diggings to find their fortune.

By the end of September 1851 there were about 10,000 people digging for gold near Ballarat. By 1852, the news had spread to England, Europe, China and America, and boatloads of people arrived in Melbourne and headed for the goldfields. The wealthy Bendigo goldfields were found by a woman, Margaret Kennedy, who saw gold in the creek bed in September 1851. She and a friend washed the gold using a breadmaking pan. Within a few months, there were about 20,000 people searching for gold in that area. People came from all over the world, intending to strike it rich and return home to their own countries." https://www.kidcyber.com.au/

Gold Rush

VICTORIA, now its own colony,
busy and vibrant, with prospering farming
and in 1851 the news came
'Gold found in NEW SOUTH WALES!'
'Gold found in Bendigo, in Ballarat!'
Even the most established of people left Melbourne.
Determined to find their fortune.
Police, farmers, the common man,
leaving only the elderly, the women and the children behind.

'Young Ned, why are you holding your tongue,
thinking of the words you would never have said?
Young Ned, why are you holding back tears?
You get to stay where you have been born and bred.
Young Ned, oh, why would you reject a hug?'
I thought to myself with fear in my head.
'Young Ned, stop.'
Oh, I cannot help it. I run to my father, pull him back instead.
'You must not leave! Stay with me please, oh, father!'
But this I could not say, do not beg, I had been taught.
He sat me on his knee, and he held me one last time.
I cried at the thought of him leaving; he was not yet even nine.

New South Wales, Victoria,
thriving and successful.
Creating fortunes for the people.
But the reality was not all that.
Diseases from unclean drinking water,
fighting over claims and findings.
Much too overpopulated; lack of housing,
sending people to the streets.
It was not all about the headlines in truth.

My father,
he left me when I was young.
To better our lives, to try his luck.
Slaving on the fields,
panning for gold and cleaning rocks,
for he knew there was something there...
Grazed knees from gravel, hands torn from the shovel,
But many dealt with much worse, much more.
Dysentery, typhus, sicknesses, slowly spreading.
With the rare finds of gold, came a scream of elation;
that was my father's only motivation.
Sleeping in a bed of dampened soil and hay,
in a tent with little warmth, mosquitoes a plenty,
with the little clothing he wore,
and that was shredded and torn.
But he continued.
And then, in July 1851,
a bounty reward was offered,
to whomever was first to find gold in Victoria
and the whole world kept coming.

Melbourne, chaotic.
Hotels and housing overcrowded.
Thousands staying in tents in the south.
Short supplies, soaring prices,
digging was exhausting,
foreigners came by boat,
making claims to find their fortune.
And the city of Melbourne grew rapidly.
The wealth of gold advanced Melbourne
into a metropolis.
And the richest city in the world.
"Young Ned, I'm back, how I've missed you so.
Young Ned, my boy, I had to go.
I love you my son, I hope you understand,
I did this for us, working hard on the land.
Young Ned, please forgive me for going away.
And know that you were in my prayers every day.
You need not cry, I am here for you to hold.
And now we have wealth, look, now we have gold."

Larissa Blazevski

The unfortunate gold diggers

The cities run dry
the crops run low
the people dig for gold
the old and the young
the rich and the poor
determined to strike gold
become rich
leave poverty
continue to dig
the water is turning grey
but still, they are digging
they are growing in the soil
but the gold is still there
they keep digging
they drop
and give up

James Champlin

The gold rushes

We rushed to the fields
on a horse or a bull
racing to find gold
but little did we know
who was in the bushes
they started shooting
animals went wild
fear in our eyes
they took our food
our money and tools
we had nothing but each other
we reached the fields
no free spot in sight
we started digging
we never left our hole
or it would be claimed
there were many fights
but we were all here for gold
we would dig and dig
eureka-eureka they'd whisper
as they struck gold
that made us dig
even faster and harder
day-night seven days a week

365 days a year
we found gold
we were rich
but we kept digging
we wanted more
eventually
we settled for what we had
we sold the site
and went home
we did not get robbed
we settled for a rich wealthy life.

James Champlin

The daily paper

I was a paperboy
I walked the rounds
I delivered the daily paper
the front page said
"Gold found in Ballarat"
I delivered it to 256 houses that morning
weeks went by
slowly people left their homes to find the fortune
the houses were now decreased
straight away from busy streets
to a ghost town
soon there were now homes left to deliver the paper
everything has changed by the gold rush
everyone quit to find a fortune
I was scared to walk the streets
even the police and the doctors quit
but still I delivered papers
until the day the streets run dry.

James Champlin

A Gold Dream

I dream of that shiny, glimmering gold,
then I remember, my blood freezing in the cold,
I dream of its smell – wet, earthy and rich,
then I remember, myself holed up in a ditch,
I dream of its brightness, radiating against my hand,
then I remember, gripping dull, muddy land,
I dream of eating gold, soft, nutty, creamy gold,
then I remember, it's just bread mould,
I dream of gold, clutched tightly in my hand,
then I remember, what I hold isn't grand.
Gold!!! I yell,
then I remember, what I have would not sell,
I dream of gold, warming my skin,
then I remember, all I have is the hair on my chin,
I dream and dream,
of a gold's gleam,
but in the end, it is just that.
A dream.

Antonio Bentovski

The Aboriginal Spirit of Melbourne

The Wurundjeri people
called Melbourne their perfect place.
Gold took over in utter disgrace,
once a sanctuary of union,
ruined by the gold bullion.
Greed destroyed many friendships,
all for a glimpse of nugget chips.
White parents losing their life,
ruined in the mines of strife.
Wurundjeri life destroyed, stolen and abducted,
the thirst for gold, ruinous and protracted.
Don't they know it is so?
Yet they look and search for it,
in rivers, in mines, in the ground,
searching desperately dug outs,
a few have found gold,
yet many, hundreds, thousands, search with doubt.
The Australian Gold Rush
brought a lot of wealth
but ruined a native culture with stealth.

Antonio Bentovski

Melbourne, Princess Bridge looking west towards Falls Bridge, 1860

Swanston Street, Melbourne, 1858

1854
Eureka Stockade

Peter Lalor, by Ludwig Becker,
National Library of Australia obj-137404456

Prompted by the digger's opposition of miners' licences, the Eureka Stockade was a twenty-minute battle which took place on 3rd December 1854 in Ballarat. The event is seen as the birthplace of Australian democracy. In the aftermath, gold licences were abolished and replaced by the Miner's Right.

On 30 November 1854, miners from the Victorian town of Ballarat, disgruntled with the way the colonial government had been administering the goldfields, swore allegiance to the Southern Cross flag at Bakery Hill and built a stockade at the nearby Eureka diggings. The charismatic Irishman Peter Lalor became the leader of the protest and led the diggers to the area around Eureka. Early on the morning of Sunday 3 December, when the stockade was only lightly guarded, government troops attacked. At least 22 diggers and six soldiers were killed. Eureka is a significant event in the development of Australia's representational structures and attitudes towards democracy and egalitarianism."

National Museum of Australia

Swearing Allegiance to the Southern Cross, watercolour by Charles A Doudiet, 1 December 1854. Art Gallery of Ballarat

Peter Lalor Speaks

The rebellion was a brutal battle,
against unfair taxes of work,
and among the fighters,
was Peter Lalor, a brave and fearless hero,
he inspired many miners, diggers, and stonemasons,
to rise and fight for their rightful revolution,
a leader of the Eureka Stockade rebellion,
who fought for truth, justice, and fairness,
for democracy and the rights of people,
to not pay taxes when they do not work,
and for this, he lost an arm,
he lost friend the hail of police bullets.
But he gained respect, love, and admiration,
years later, a street was named after him,
his dedication, bravery and fearlessness,
forever remembered,
however, Peter Lalor remembers his heroes.
He remembers the twenty — two killed miners,
who sacrificed their lives for the good of all.
He invites their wives and children to his home
to unite, to share a meal to remember the dead heroes.
And then, Peter Lalor speaks:

"Do not weep because you have lost your husbands and
fathers,
feel victorious and proud, for what your brave men achieved.
They changed the law, changed the taxes, established
democracy!!!!!
Be proud and honour their sacrifices, as I do.
They are heroes, and will be forever recognised and never
forgotten,
their names, forever written in history!!!
Amen."

Antonio Bentovski

Eureka Stockade

Within walls of wood, painted red blood on beige,
a grudge between rivals, caused reason for rage.
The soldiers and diggers, in a stockade was war,
in strife were the miners who had not a wage.

Miners, with no justice, punished unfairly,
for each could not mine without paying every penny.
A mining license was given to those with money,
the digging was harsh meaning very little the earnings of many.

Whoever took the risk to mine without consent,
was penalized and tied up until they paid every cent.

Whatever were to happen didn't matter anymore,
for they built a stockade, marched in unison, with force.

A rough disagreement, an unfair law, miners with no choice,
they vow for rights, but the soldiers' bullets aim at their sites.

The licenses are dead, because of the miners' sacrifice,
Peter Lalor is shot but Liberty is born and finds her voice.

Larissa Blazevski

April 21, 1856 — Melbourne Stonemasons Win the Eight-Hour Working Day

On 26 March 1856, workers called a public meeting at the Queen's Theatre, in Melbourne, to make a stand on improving working conditions. At the meeting it was announced that 'the time has arrived when the system of 8 hours should be introduced into the building trades and that after the 21st of the next month we promise to work 8 hours and no longer'.

Negotiations between the union and the building companies broke down and on 21 April 1856, stonemasons, led by James Stephens, downed tools at the construction site of the law faculty buildings at Melbourne University and walked off the job.

As Stephens said, 'It was a burning hot day and I thought the occasion a good one, so I called upon the men to follow me, to which they immediately consented, when I marched them ... to Parliament House'.

Stonemasons from other construction sites along the way joined the march.

It was thereby agreed that stonemasons would work an eight-hour day. The campaign placed Australia as a front runner in the campaign for human rights and is now commemorated with the Labour Day public holidays.

National Museum of Australia

James Stevens

Eight-hour day banner, Melbourne, 1856

Thomas Topping

The Eight Stonemasons of Melbourne

Eight hours,
the power of protest granted us these eight glorious hours
of rest,
of recreation
A reprieve from the ruinous work that weighed us down.
There is a myriad of stonemasons,
but the number eight is all that matters,
all that gives us sublime meaning.
We were many,
but we were Eight,
we gave the whole world a happier day.

Chloe Falzon

Together We Stand

Together we stand in unity,
united fighting for a life of dignity,
the freedom to be respected and treated as one.
Together we stand,
faces towards our future,
flying high and proud, the faded image of humanity.
Together we stand,
a ring around equality,
standing strong for what we all believe in.
Together we stand,
ignited by their greed
bolstered by their brute force.
Together we stand,
a united ring surrounding our dreams,
the bravery to give the people the right to be people.
Together we stand,
strong with each other,
fighting until we cannot fight any longer.
Together we stand.

Cecilia Bingham

1858 — Melbourne
Mother of Aussie Football

In 1857, Tom Wills, one of the founders of Australian Football, returned to Melbourne after schooling in England where he was football captain of Rugby School and a brilliant cricketer. Initially, he advocated the winter game of football as a way of keeping cricketers fit during off-season.

The new game was devised by Wills, his cousin H.C.A. Harrison, W.J. Hammersley and J.B. Thompson. The Melbourne Football Club was formed on August 7, 1858 – the year of the code's first recorded match between Scotch College and Melbourne Grammar School.

The game quickly blossomed. The Geelong Football Club was formed in 1859 and in 1866 an updated set of rules was put in place and competition started.

The Victorian Football League was established in 1896 and the following year the League's first games were played among the foundation clubs – Carlton, Collingwood, Essendon, Fitzroy, Geelong, Melbourne, St Kilda and South Melbourne.

In 1908, Richmond and University joined the competition. But after the 1914 season, University left the League. In 1925, Footscray (now the Western Bulldogs), Hawthorn and North Melbourne joined the VFL. https://aflinternational.com/history/

Melbourne Football Club, 1879

It feels like magic

It is electric,
when you touch that ball,
that rough skin,
grating against your fingers.

It is like lightning,
shooting up your veins,
when you drop it onto your foot,
and kick it to your heart's content.

It feels like fire,
every time you put that guernsey on,
the number lights up your back,
and puts fight into your bones.

It feels like ice,
when those very same bones shatter,
taking your hopes in the process,
nothing but desire to feel the ball again left.

But then it feels like gold,
when you are back on the field,
running, leaping, kicking,
surrounded by brothers and the crashing wind.

And then the gold becomes molten,
coating you in euphoria,
when that final siren blows,
and your team's points stack up the most.

Chloe Falzon

Melbourne Mother of Aussie Football

"By golly, I've got it"
Tom Wills spoke:
"In Winter's time, in the off season of cricket,
we'll play a game of what I call footy.
It's like football, but it's an Australian Rules Football.
With this, we'll keep warm and fit during the bitter cold,
and have fun and enjoyment, while having a kick with our mates.
The game will consist of twenty players, and the ball, an oval shaped possum skinned ball.
This will create tension, excitement and a new challenge to the traditional sport.
We'll play on a new modified cricket pitch, with four poles on either side for goals.
Kick the goal in between the middle posts, simply receive six points, kick it in the between the other posts? One point.
How about that?"
Then the whole room roared with cheers and celebrations.

5 August 1879, Melbourne Cricket Ground, Collingwood Rifles vs East Melbourne Artillery.
As I walk out of the dressing rooms,
I hear the roaring crowd,

I feel the wet grass beneath me,
the wind blowing against my face,
I see the banners flying high,
sweat is running down my face,
blood is fiercely pumping my veins,
the referee signals play,
the game has begun.

After the game, at the pub
instead of heading home, everyone gathered around the pub. To have laughs drinks and jokes.
"Did you see Will's kick? Must have been from 40 meters out."
"More than that mate!"
"The game looks rather fun; it makes Winter appealing now"
"It sure keeps us fit and healthy for cricket"
"What'd you think Tom?"
Tom Wills speaks:
"Some may squabble or argue or even fight about the result or the umpire's decision, but AFL is more than that.
It's more than keeping fit for cricket, more than winning and losing.
It is about having fun!!!
Bringing people and individuals together!
Making new friends, having a kick, playing together,
that's what it's about.
Gathering around together as we all are at this very moment,
discussing the game, laughing at jokes,
This is what it makes OUR football special!!!!!!!!!!"
Once again, the pub roared in cheers and then exclaimed:

"God bless you Tom Wills, and God bless the Australian Rules Football."

This is how Tom Wills created the Australian spirit of mateship!

Antonio Bentovski

Melbourne Mother of Football

Melbourne –Mother of football,
you called upon Tom Wills.
For celebration of your youth
with a new pastime.
A dead possum, its skin, oval shaped,
twenty-two men; volunteers,
a field of mud.
A ball, bouncing in any direction
and players kicking goals,
Entertainment for all of Melbourne.
Regardless of the biting wind,
the sodden leather boots,
the crowd; nestled under the shelter of umbrellas.
And chanting at opposing ends.
The scores level,
the pressure rising,
our quickening breath.
Unity, goodwill,
brotherhood.
A game of action,
and entertainment for all of Melbourne to enjoy.

Larissa Blazevski

A different kind of victory

The roar of the crowd erupted through the open field,
children, of all shapes and sizes,
had gathered from many different parts of the growing city,
to get a peek of the action,
their curiosity growing,
such a foreign concept conceived right at home,
they waited to see if they could join in.
The cold rain soaked the earth and the surrounding watchers,
it slapped the muddy ground as it raced down from the dark gloomy sky,
yet it did not stop the burning passion from the young players.
They rocketed across the slippery floor chasing the mysterious jewel,
brown dull yet as precious as the stones on a woman's neck.
Yelling across the field,
the sounds of wind and water rushing across their face,
the adrenalin coursing through their blood like a rushing river,
they ran.
A small boy ran forward with all his might,
swerving left and right,
following its unpredictable path,
silence from the sidelines as they waited for what would happen next,
he reached out forward and lunged.

The uproar of the crowed echoed through the wind as the ball was caught.
He ran,
through the harsh rain and squelchy mud,
this feeling,
he could never feel it anywhere else,
he felt free,
free from all the troubles of the world,
this was a victory even if they didn't win.

Cecilia Bingham

1853 – 1860 — University of Melbourne, State Library of Victoria, National Gallery of Victoria

The State Library Victoria is the central library of the State of Victoria, Australia, located in Melbourne. It was established in 1854 as the Melbourne Public Library, making it Australia's oldest public library and one of the first free libraries in the world.

Melbourne Public Library's Domed Reading Room was commissioned to celebrate the library's jubilee, in 1913

The Spirit of Early Melbourne

Melbourne's gold rush built a new city.
Riches and people shaped Melbourne's future.
The quiet and disputed settlement
turned to a thriving and vibrant town.
Talented British architects
drawing inspiration from home
creating magnificent architecture
in the endeavour to build up the best new city.
Forming a society to provide culture and education.

Grand and ornate buildings,
embracing places from afar
such as the State Library,
with its grand dome,
the Treasury building,
housing the abundance of gold.
Churches to practise faith.
Theatres and galleries introducing culture.
Libraries opening a world of knowledge.
Free Schools and Universities unlocking one's mind.

Larissa Blazevski

1860 – 1861 — Expedition by Burke and Wills to cross Australia from Melbourne to the Gulf of Carpentaria

Robert O'Hara Burke, William John Wills, John King and Charles Gray became the first Europeans to cross Australia south to north when they reached the Gulf of Carpentaria in February 1861. The expedition's departure from Royal Park, Melbourne on 20 August 1860 was a public spectacle watched by about 15,000 people.

The death of Burke, Wills and Charles Gray during their return led the expedition to be mythologised in Australian culture as a heroic failure. It ultimately prompted the discovery of vast grazing lands, enabling further European settlement of the interior. National Museum of Australia

Burke and Wills, 1862, wood engraving, unknown artist

Departure of the Expedition by A.H. Massina & Co

Deserving more than Death

Diamond Poems

Life
Adventures, Unforeseen,
Successes, Journeys, Cross-roads,
Learning, Growing, Searching, Lost,
Stopping, Condemned, Misery,
Dying, Decaying,
Glory

Burke
Brave, Explorer,
Daring, Crossing, Australia,
Wiling, Sacrifice,
Young, Surveyor,
Wills

Antonio Bentovski

Burke and Wills speak

On camels, we left
guided by Afghan cameleers,
and men on twenty-two willing horses
for on an expedition
heading from south to north of Australia
the reward less important
than our bravery.
From the friendly eucalyptus trees,
to the unfriendly weather and scurvy,
our grazed and sore knees,
our road was aghast
our future seemed very far,
yet so close in the power of our mind.

Our movements swift
death our enemy too large to grip.
Waiting for supplies,
a month's wait; restless and breathless.
Impatience takes over.
Notes; written and engraved in bark,
attempts to guide the men in the dark,
avoiding the searing heat
and the stones burning our feet.
The few who bought supplies for us,

pushed us on our route
travelling fast and far
reaching the Gulf of Carpentaria!
Visions of supplies and visions of return
never once did left our exhausted minds.
Yet we embraced the land
as if it were our last chance
to ride it on horseback.
We continued the journey of returning
but Wills was growing weak
and my eyes were burning
seeking help
and water
and food
we lost communication
we lost every eatable ration
Burke died a horrible death.
We mourned, but we continued
we weren't far from the awaiting reward.
Soon, I felt as if I was dragging my feet along,
as if an imaginary hand was pushing me onwards.
I was weak too
I lay next to a waterhole.
I knew that King would survive alone.
I lay freezing and slightly lightheaded,
trying to grasp the life I had
but it slowly left me.
Burke and wills are angels now.
They are still exploring our humanity now.

Larissa Blazevski

1872 — Free Education for All, The First Public School in the World commences in Melbourne

On the 17th of December 1872, the Victorian Government passed the Education Act 1872. The Premier, James Francis, reformed the education system along the lines of the 1866 Royal Commission.

The legislation made Victoria the first Australian colony (and one of the first jurisdictions in the world) to offer free, secular and compulsory education to its children. Under the new law, children between the ages of six and 15 were obliged to attend school and their education was free.

Charles H. Pearson, education reformer: "I need not here go over the old ground that an educated community is on the whole moral, more law abiding and more capable of work than an uneducated one." https://www.vic.gov.au/150-years-public-education-victoria-media-kit

The newly established Education Office, Melbourne, 1872

Souvenir of the Golden Jubilee of Free Education, Victoria, 1922

Front of the Doncaster Primary School with the Doncaster Tower and the Tower Hotel in the distance. The pupils are assembled with Mr A. O. Thiele the Headmaster. There appears to be about 56 boys and 34 girls, and also two lady teachers. DP0079, Doncaster Templestowe Historical Society

Melton Primary School was originally the State-subsidised Combined Denomination School, which was opened on 17th May 1858, with an attendance of about 30 children. In 1863, when Melton was a staging post for Cobb & Co. coaches, the school was declared a Common School and received its number, 430.

Free Education for All

A speech presented by Charles Henry Pearson.

"Is it fair for education to have a price?
Is it fair to exclude others due to their gender, religion or race, or perhaps wealth?
It is fair to have a religious school, and not a public one?"
This is what Charles H. Pearson questioned.
"If the word of God, and the word of the Bible is to "love thy neighbour, as thy love thy self" or perhaps be "inclusive" and "forgive sinners and be merciful", then why are we excluding others due to their different religion, or their financial status?
Shouldn't education be free for all!!
Shouldn't education be a right to access to all!!!
Shouldn't we speak up?
Shouldn't we inspire others?
Shouldn't we influence and change?
This is not justice,
this is not democracy,
this is dictatorship,
a tyranny !!!!!!!!!
Who will side with us, the unknown people?"
We do not have any power, support, or strength,
cried the crowd.
"Justice, fairness, and God.

If we fight,
will the Church take actions to silence us?
Will the government of Melbourne side with the Church
or the people?
Will the people see the ugly side of this injustice?
Education only for the rich?
The cruelty, the prejudices, the bigotries.
Religious schools should be free,
Government schools should be free,
leaders should be preaching freedom,
not exclusion.
Imagine a world of free teachers and free students!
A free career, a free religious path for all children to take,
guided by the teachers!!
Let us fight people, Australians, Melburnians, for a free,
independent,
secular school, let us not rest until we succeed,
for justice, for fairness, for Melburnians, for our children,
for a ***free education.****"*

Antonio Bentovski

1901 — Australian Federation commences in Melbourne

The Commonwealth of Australia was inaugurated on 1st January 1901 in Centennial Park, Sydney. In March, elections were held for the new Federal Parliament, and in May the celebrations focused on Melbourne, where the first Federal Parliament was opened in the (Royal) Exhibition Building.

The First Commonwealth Parliament was opened by the Duke of York in the Exhibition Building, Melbourne, on 9 May, 1901

The Exhibition Building was built for the first International Trade Exhibition, held between 1 October — 30 April 1881.

The Creators

How can you live,
when you know nothing?
How can you live,
when you exist unaware
of those before you
who created everything
you hold dear?
The answer is,
you cannot.
That is why we must learn.
Oh, we must learn with the ferocity
of those brave people
who dared to put their lives at risk,
for the common good,
for us.

Chloe Falzon

Federation Celebrations, 'Opening of the First Parliament of the Commonwealth', Exhibition Building, Melbourne, 9th May 1901

Elizabeth Street, Melbourne

1914
The ANZACS

ANZAC

"When war broke out in 1914 Australia had been a federated nation for only 13 years, and its government was eager to establish a reputation among the nations of the world. When Britain declared war in August 1914 Australia was automatically placed on the side of the Commonwealth. In 1915 Australian and New Zealand soldiers formed part of the expedition that set out to capture the Gallipoli peninsula in order to open the Dardanelles to the allied navies. The ultimate objective was to capture Constantinople (now Istanbul), the capital of the Ottoman Empire, an ally of Germany."
Australian War Memorial

ANZAC prisoners of war from the Gallipoli Campaign

Lieutenant (Lt) **Claude Henry Vautin**, *Australian Flying Corps (AFC), from Yuin, Western Australia, Lt* **Stanley Rubert Jordan**, *9th Battalion, from Lismore, N.S.W., Captain (Capt)* **Thomas Walter White**, *AFC from Melbourne, Victoria, and Lt* **Leslie Henry Luscombe**, *14th Battalion from Geelong, Victoria.*

George W. Handsley, 2nd Australian Light Horse Regiment. He was captured at the Suez Canal, in August 1915 and spent two and half years as a prisoner of war. Read his book ***Two-and-a-Half Years a Prisoner of War in Turkey*** *found at the site of the National Library of Australia. https://nla.gov.au/nla.obj-38438001/view?partId=nla.obj-38438017#page/n0/mode/1up*

ANZAC soldier prisoner of the Turks

George Handsley joined the Light Horse Brigade
he dreamed of fighting for his country
his dream turned to a nightmare
he's never been out of Queensland
he yearned to see the world
never he imagined he would be a prisoner of war!

From Suffolk, England, to Sohag, Egypt,
in sandy dunes he trains
the 2nd Light Horse troops
ride like winds in the sandy plains.

He fought with the enemy in battles big and fierce
he saw the men suffer akin with the horses
George and his regiment frequently looked
for the wild tribes of Bedouins
who plagued the countryside.
They had several close escapes from capture
due to surprise attacks
and needing to rely heavily on their mounts.
There was the one time he was on foot,
he failed to escape being captured by the Turks.

AT DAWN CAME MY DEFEAT,
as soon as there was light
the enemy made a series of sharp attacks
both flank and front
shot at, caught, and trapped.

For two and a half years a prisoner,
in the dark, and vicious years of the war.

Questioned harshly by the enemy
we spat in disgust surprisingly not shot,
taken again, to another one of their spots
little water, no food
yet questions again
still, we refuse
for we don't want to hear our buddies' funeral songs.
Now, we may hear ours, is what I thought.
When men came cocking their rifles
most likely dawning our funeral songs
the song would have played
yet, it did not
for a German officer who spoke rather quickly
holding our songs

Then came the evening on this day of capture
told to drink from the well but not given food
stoned and spat at
in the local town
on a trip we call hell.

When not moving on the cattle truck
we were treated like cattle
and put to hard labour.
Only in Jerusalem did we get to eat
real soup and meat,
our heads shaved
then onwards to Damascus
paraded around the street
like cattle again,
laughed at and stones thrown at us,
then in the truck onwards to Aleppo
incarcerated with Turks, Armenians, Greeks
and others who refused to take up arms.
Another journey to Ismaile
where we are forced to walk up the mountains
hike through darkness,
sleep in the open,
feeling hungry and frozen.

Early dawn another march and the same hunger
being almost dead
we reached Affion-Cara-Hissar.
Fed a small loaf and half a pint of boiled wheat
twice a day, like horses in a farm
getting flogged daily for the slightest things
thrashing words, we don't understand,
then again forced to work
chopping wood for the strong
building roads for the meek men
dressed in worn out boots, feet bleeding,

bags tied around our feet, not helping.

Cruelty has no end
100 prisoners all flogged
for a Turk religious festival
that forbids us to eat anything at all,
no food given to us
we complain, no food, no work,
we are flogged again and again,
they must think we feel no pain.

I survived and sailed home South
coming home to Brisbane on April 1st.
This was hell on earth, not an adventure,
I experienced pain and torture,
two and a half hellish years
an ANZAC prisoner of the Turks.

Divinia Kihara

George Handsley Anzac Prisoner

George Handsley thought this would be a great idea; going to war was going to be the best adventure he had ever been on. He knew he was good at horse riding so signing up for the Light Horse Regiment was going to be even more exciting.

After finishing his training on the deserts of Egypt, he boarded the Australian *Suffolk*. He met up with his 2nd Light Horse Regiment in Sohag, on the west bank of the Nile in Egypt. Being placed in battles and seeing many perish; he believed that horses deserved more recognition for their dedication.

On one fateful battle where his stallion was not with him, he ended up being a prisoner. George was captured on the 4th of August 1916, at the Battle of Romani, Egypt, during a sudden and sharp attack by the Turks. Prior to this event, George had been shot on his left arm and momentarily fell unconscious. Regaining consciousness, George bandaged his wound, grabbed his rifle, and re-joined the battle in minutes.

Looking at where he now stood, he only saw sergeant Drysdale along with trooper McColl. The realisation hit all of them; they were the only Brits among Turks, they were outnumbered. Not long after they became prisoners.

All three of them were taken to a German officer who interrogated them on their troop numbers and weapons. All three being faithful gave up no useful information. Irritated by their stubbornness, the officer cursed and spat.

They then marched the prisoners through a desert all the way to Katea. Once reaching their destination, they were greeted with soldiers all armed with rifles. They asked the three Brits to share their secrets and information but again like last time, they refused.

That same evening George, Drysdale and McColl were bound with ropes and continued their journey without knowing where they were being led.

After finding out that their destination was Ber Ol-Ald, the prisoners were allowed to drink from an unsanitary well but were given no food. After getting water they were met with regiments of Bedouins who were on top of camels. Their faces were hostile and ready to attack. Entering any town was a cause for trouble, they were often welcomed with stones and saliva aimed their way.

Travelling on weak camels for some time, they were transferred to a rundown railway, drawn by donkeys, as far as Raffia. From there they were taken to a cattle truck.

The cattle truck was as cramped and unsanitary. The truck was so cramped, George and his comrades had to crouch down, heads in between their legs. They were given a packet of hard biscuits and a few dates which were confiscated by their escort. The wound on George's hand had not been attended to causing great discomfort and pain. In addition, all three soldiers had caught a bad case of dysentery.

After a day and night of travelling, they all reached Jerusalem where they had their first proper meal in days. After filling their bellies up, a Turkish barber came and shaved their heads and faces.

They then headed back into the same filthy cattle truck where they were put on display for the locals to see. As one could imagine, their welcome was filled with stones, faeces, and other disgusting rubbish.

72 hours later, they were again in the same cattle truck and on their way to Aleppo where they joined others just like them, prisoners who were from rival nations or people who refused to take part in war.

Their next adventure would be to go to Ismaile and climb over the mountains. The view was wonderful, and they would have enjoyed it if they had been there on different circumstances. The landscape seemed fertile and filled with hearty fruits and vegetables.

They hiked through the night and soon camped in the open greenery. Once the sun had finally risen, they continued their trek, stomachs empty. Any pleas and cries for food were responded with sly expressions and toothy grins. It drove the hostages insane to see their captors sneering at their desperation.

As more prisoners arrived, the numbers went up to 39. This caused a problem as they were heading to Affiom – Cara – Hisser in another cattle truck.

George started doubting if he could last for the entire journey that they were taken. On the morning of August 27, 23 days after George Handsley had been taken hostage by the Turks, the prisoners were taken to a camp in which they were able to take a bath and again had their heads shaved. Each person was placed into a cramped room called the quarantine room, and stayed in this room for 14 days, their meals consisting of a small loaf of bread and a half pint of boiled wheat twice daily.

Prisoners were regularly whipped for the most irrelevant things or for offences the prisoners themselves were ignorant to.

In the camp, everyone was assigned duties such as chopping wood or road building. The equipment given to them were not reliable and their boots were full of holes by this stage. The prisoners put bags on top of their boots to stop further wounds to their feet.

After a while, one hundred and fifty of the prisoners were chosen to work on the railway line that went between Angora and Sebastopol. These men made their way to the station at Affion – Cara – Hissar. They were then loaded onto trucks and mentally prepared themselves for long hours, poor meals, and filthy working areas and overcrowded quarters.

George and the other prisoners were often frozen cold as the weather at the camp was always freezing and miserable. They even had to work on Christmas Day when the snow was all the way up to their knees.

Trooper Handsley recollects a moment during the stay in which one hundred inmates were flogged. On this occasion, it was by Turkish religion forbidden to eat bread, because of this, no ration was sent to the inmates, and this caused the majority of the prisoners to refuse working as they would not be receiving food. The commandant of the camp commanded to flog all those who denied working.

George Handsley survived by luck or by strength or by both luck and strength. He made it back to Australia with little damage done to his mental and physical health. Once the war had ended, he was directly taken to England, at Sutton Veny, convalescent camp, to recover. On February 22nd, 1919, he sailed his way back to Australia, on the Transport "Ascanius". George felt that sailing back home had replenished him. He landed on Brisbane on the 1st of April 1919.

Sandra Panamthathu

The Warzone

I see the sandy shores
I hear orders from the Lieutenant
Think fast, act immediately, live another day.
I feel the waves, crashing and splashing on my face,
I taste the sweat, salt upon my lips,
I smell the fear.
Then I see soldiers falling like flies,
I hear the anguish, bone – chilling screams,
I feel my heart, throbbing against my throat,
I taste the blood, splattered across my face,
I smell poison, a mixture of blood, dirt, and gunpowder.
Bang!
Then I see my blood painting the yellow and grainy sand
bright red,
I hear my heart stopping,
I feel my legs give in, falling ... forever,
I smell the wet sand, covered in my blood,
I taste blood in my throat,
Then I see, nothing.

Antonio Bentovski

Captain Robert Bage (1888 - 1915)

Lieutenant Bage enlisted in the AIF in 1914.

Bob Bage, member of the First Australasian Antarctic Expedition

Melbourne Engineer Robert Bage took part in Douglas Mawson's Australasian Antarctic Expedition 1911-14. During WWI he volunteered and was subsequently killed in May 1915, the second week of the Gallipoli Campaign.

Bob was born in Melbourne on the 18th of April 1888. After graduating in Civil Engineering, Bob Bage joined the militia in 1909 and two years later transferred, as an officer, to the Royal Australian Engineers. In 1911, he obtained leave of absence, without pay, and joined the Australasian Antarctic Expedition, under Sir Douglas Mawson, as astronomer, assistant magnetician (specialising in magnetism) and recorder of tides.

On 10 November 1912, Capt. Bage was leader of the southern sledging party, together with the New Zealand magnetician Eric Webb, and the photographer Frank Hurley. They accomplished a perilous journey of 600 miles, man-hauling their sledge over rough blizzard swept ice surfaces, in order to study the extent of the South Magnetic Pole region. He afterwards contributed the chapter entitled ***"The Quest of the Southern Magnetic Pole"*** *to Sir Douglas Mawson's book* ***The Home of the Blizzards****. He was to have received the Polar Medal, lately awarded by the King George V.*

When the 1st Australian Army Division for service abroad was formed, he volunteered for active service and was appointed second in command of the 3rd Field Company (Engineers), with the rank of captain. He took part in the landing at ANZAC on 25 April 1915. Twelve days later he was sent to an exposed position to peg out a new trench line. He came under intense machine-gun fire and was repeatedly hit. His dead body could not be recovered until dark; he was later buried in the Beach Cemetery at ANZAC.

Bob Bage Speaks

Whoosh, the wind blows flowing through my body
chills creeping up my chest for my quest begins.
Step by step my mind fills with curiosity
what my discovery will be today,
my face turned towards the South Pole.
Inordinate winds and snow brushes against my body
but hope is laying in my heart waiting to be found.
1,000-kilometre journey
while being trapped in the wintry Antarctic
secluded from the outside world,
feeling lost with only one way out
hits differently when you think about it.
My adventurous skills are set in motion
well, adventure runs through my blood.
I believe that every single person
on the face of the planet
has one simple job,
to serve and
be willing to face the challenges of the world.
My friend explorers and I were faithful
in exploring the undiscovered areas of Antarctica.
Eric Webb, a fellow civil engineer from New Zealand,
makes me feel I have a brother and a father,
standing by me, ensuring me, showing me the way

to keep on, march on, bring the South Pole to the world.
Frank Hurley, the brave photographer from Sydney,
I learn from his bravery, I gain from his mastery,
his strength is immeasurable, his brotherhood memorable.
We made it through the eye-piercing winds,
the skin splitting blizzards!
We brought the South Pole to the world!
And finally, the day had come
where our ship was ready to take us back to our dwellings.
But my heart was alerted to save a soul who was part of my soul,
my dear Mawson was missing,
my leader and mentor lost in the ice and the winds hissing.
Our dear comrades Ninnis and Mertz were with Mawson,
we loved them the same,
we would never abandon them.
I stayed back with others to save their dear life,
but we were unable to save all crew members.
Almost broken, Mawson emerged lonely, alone,
from the blinding snow.
Another winter in the Antarctic
and then heading home, sweet home!

Life had to change with war
with my back turned behind on my discoveries
I went back to things I knew how to do well.
My army engineers were calling me again
As I had arrived back from my expedition.
A war had started from eye to eye
I was not going to give into letting the other country win.
I'm a natural leader nothing goes down on my watch,
especially my land.

I was recruited in the AIF second in command,
and I was unbothered since I am a humble young man
working on landing in ANZAC on April 25th 1915.
12 days later I was exposed in a highly unshielded area
an area blocked from the outer world,
a dusty and vague place
I was dazed in the moment
as I was shot unaware of the distant guns.
My body was not found until later that day
I was buried six feet under
at Anzac cemetery bay in Gallipoli.
My loved ones
I shall not return
but my life flashed right
before my eyes
that was the end of Bob Bage,
now I regret the decision I made,
I feel like I made a blind decision,
instead of leaving a legacy,
I ended quite abruptly,
the whole world was there in my hands
and I decided to let go.

May your soul rest in peace innocent soul
they still look for you
and will never forget you
at the South Pole.
There is still life inside you innocent soul
Bob Bage, 1888-1915.

Janelle Kauseni

Douglas Mawson and Bob Bage

T*hree days,* he thought to himself. *Three days. "Wait for me for five days, and if don't show, wait another three. If I'm not back, I am probably buried 6 feet under the snow."* Three days had passed eight days ago. And yet there was still no sign of Douglas Mawson, or his crew. The rest of the crew have already left, taking most of their provisions and supplies with them back to their long journey home, Australia, leaving Bob alone with five other volunteers to fend for themselves.

In Antarctica.

They had left them with a decent supply of provisions, thankfully. A sack full of apples, a few oatcakes and half a keg of salted beef for him to eat, a spare map, tools and equipment. They had even managed to spare Bob a boat, should he find Mawson and the rest of the missing team.

Bob looked at his pocket watch. It was noon, the sun at its peak, yet you couldn't tell from the way the sun hid behind the clouds, like a cub would hide behind its mother. You'd think it was dusk. The clouds cast a looming shadow, the winds soared, and Bob with his men, was the only living thing in sight for a hundred miles in the middle of this frozen wasteland. He spent his days with at the abandoned camp, hoping for Mawson's arrival. He ate. He slept. He dreamed. And he hoped, all while slowly feeling exhausted. Yet he kept at his work, his mission.

He sat in his tent, with a half-drawn map laid out in front of him. It was a map of Antarctica. It had all the mountains and rivers and lakes that he and his expedition explored, with a mapping of the stars and creatures they had encountered. He continued to draw and sketch and map, awaiting Mawson's arrival. It was his duty after all, and his passion; to explore the unknown and learn about the great gift of life and of nature. He spent hours upon hours in his tent, with about a dozen maps, re-sketching the plains and learning about Antarctica's new time zones. He hadn't seen or read about this before. The time was different to that of Melbourne, with the sun rising and setting earlier. He had thought it to be from the magnetic fields of Antarctica and the idea that it was the southernmost territory on Earth. However, Mawson proposed the stars had a part to play and their alignment in certain parts of the world. I guess they would never know.

Bob carefully set aside the fragile maps and then took out his journal to read over it. It was an old leather-bound journal gifted to him by his parents, before he left for Antarctica. It wasn't much, but it held great importance to him. This is how he spent his time, reading and writing of the wonders that Antarctica beholds. Bob read over the adventures he had with his friends, visiting lakes and oceans and mountains unknown to man. He read over his scientific notations to better understand Antarctica and its magnetic fields and star locations. He read over his journal, page by page, to pass the time.

He was up to the part where he and his team had discovered a mountain, tainted with iron-oxide saltwater, which they had named the 'blood falls', when his stomach then rumbled. Bob had been nelly starving himself in hope to reserve the food they were left with for as long as possible. He was feeling responsible to save food for his group. He had eaten very little in nearly two days. He looked like a different man since his arrival in Antarctica, all frail and weak and thin. Once he stepped foot outside the tent, a huge wind then breezed over him which sent a shiver down his spine. It was starting to get colder than when he first arrived here eight months ago. The snow had also risen too. It was at his ankles, yet now it sat just below his knees. Shivering, he headed towards the keg, sinking with each step. Once he managed to crawl to the keg, he moved the wooden lid. The stench that was released was among the foulest he had ever breathed. Bob wretched vomit that coloured the snow a sickening green. The meat had spoiled, all mould-eaten and off colour.

Great he thought to himself. There was his only reliable food supply, all rotten and spoiled. His worries started to grow on him now. If he did not die from hunger, the cold would get him. Or the bears. Or the seals. Or the abominable snowman for all he knew.

He hadn't left his camp since the day the other crew left. It was too dangerous. Yet he had to leave now and hunt. He couldn't survive only on apples. He headed back inside his tent and opened his chest that sat at the foot of his bed. As he rummaged through it, he set all his rifles and revolvers aside. Bob was too clever to fall into that trap. Should he shoot his target, the gunshots will spook any game within the radius of hundreds of miles. He instead reached for his bow and his quiver, loaded it with arrows and swung it around his head. A more silent approach was necessary. Bob peered over his shoulder and folded over one of the maps he had drawn and put it in his satchel. Should he get lost, this would lead him the way back to camp. It was better to be cautious.

Then, he left to search for food for him and his men.

Bob decided the best location to hunt would be near a water source, such as a river or a creek. Seals and swarms of krill will be widely available near the ocean, not to mention an abundance of penguins. The camp was positioned about 9 miles away from the ocean, where his boat had been sat. He re-opened his map and headed north-west past the Huey Creek (which was named after the death of crewmate Patrick "Huey" Johnson). Bob calculated it to be about a 2-hour walk.

The wind was now stronger than ever, the weather colder than ever and the snow deeper than ever. He now sank down to his thighs, and each step required an excruciating amount of energy, of which he simply did not have. Bob's stomach rumbled even louder, his breathing grew more rapid and his appetite for a slice of meat grew, his pace slowed. He then started to dream about the comforts of home, to calm his nerves.

Home.

The word was so foreign to him that he chuckled at the thought of it. It had been a while since Bob was back home, warmly dressed and fed, reading the daily edition of the paper with a cup of hot coffee. He had forgotten what home felt like, and to be well fed and slept. Bob was deep in thought when his ears picked up familiar sound. Bob looked up and managed a weak smile.

It was the sound of a single penguin squawking.

The penguin was about three-quarters of his size, 16 feet away from him, happily gulping the handful of fish it had managed to scavenge. Bob very carefully and very silently drew his bow and arrow and aimed at the penguin. He let it loose, killing it swiftly, cleanly, and silently. It had dropped to the ground with a thump, its bright red blood steaming the ice and snow. Still smiling, what an irony, Bob ran towards the penguin and began dragging the dead penguin back to base camp to feed himself and his volunteer men. Once the penguin was all skinned and butchered and the fire running, barely, he began to cook the slices. As he rotated the slices on his knife left and right, Bob and his men began licking their lips hungrily, as a tiger would upon its prey. This penguin had single-handedly appeased their hunger and boosted their morale. Not only would they be sufficiently fed for a few days, but the fish would last a good while between now and his next hunt.

As Bob and the men were halfway finished into devouring the penguin, they heard a familiar voice:

"Got any left to spare?"

Bob jerked his body around and saw a man, almost dead on his feet, with a snowy beard extending to his chest and hair past the shoulders, unrecognisable if it were not for those clothes and that voice.

It was Douglas Mawson.

Antonio Bentovski

Eric Webb[3] visits Bob Bage's grave

I remember this man like I remember my life. I realise now, that fewer than I thought still do. It's a shame what happened really, nobody thought it'd be him. Not even he thought it'd be him. I see those men, being shipped off, grins plastered on their faces, all excited about the adventure that's coming. I see those men, kissing their wife goodbye, hugging their children, and promising "I'll be back before you know it".

I see those men, drinking on the rigs, every one of them laughing heartily, as if they'd known each other for a lifetime twice over. I see those men, being gunned down before they knew they could get to the top of the hill. I see those men, with fear flashing in their eyes, the petrifying realisation of war.

Bob Bage was one of those men. I remember him, smoking that wooden pipe on the rig, coughing out blackness with each choppy bit of laughter he had. How he liked to lay awake in the middle of the night when nobody else was around, blankly staring at the stars, whispering as if he had a secret only they knew.

---

3 Eric Webb, Bob Bage and Frank Hurley were the three-man team that set out on November 10, 1912, to study the South Magnetic Pole, on a perilous journey of 600 miles using only sledges and snow dogs. They were part of the Douglas Mawson Australasian Antarctic Expedition (1911-1914).

I remember the day he enlisted; he was all sore about having to shave his beard off. He begged the commanding officer relentlessly, rambling as if he thought he'd care. Eventually, god knows how, they got him to shave it off. Although, they never could get rid of that moustache of his. I remember how he refused to wear his shoes right, there's not been one time I saw him with the laces done up correctly. Countless other soldiers would ask if they could tie them, he even fell over the bloody things once. Yet, Bob blatantly refused to do them up. Flashback to the Antarctic when we had no laces for a snow boots, only strong stings to tie around them and never looking down at them, always looking up at the stars that guided us to the South Pole. Who knows who this Bob is, in Gallipoli? Who knows what science and what astronomy and what humanity they have killed?

I remember how he used to lecture the other soldiers about constellations, every night describing what he saw. You could tell by the way other soldiers looked at him, the way their eyes became unfocused, that they couldn't understand. How could they? Their minds were running, fuelled with gunpowder and the thought of adventure. Running to the battlefields they were desperate for.

It was more than obvious, yet Bob wouldn't give up on them. No, that didn't fit his character. His lectures continued regardless, another quiet night, another lecture from Bob. He reminisced with them, recounting stories from his days in the Antarctic, him, and Douglas Mawson. How the stars guided his way through the biting cold, telling how each bright light painted the map of the skies.

You could tell by the look in his eyes Bob Bage admired the

stars. He was like a man starving for stars, he desired them. No, he craved them. It'd be absurd to think one-day Bob would stop gazing at the constellations.

It's a wonder how he became a lieutenant. The day I heard it my jaw dropped open. Oh, how that gazer grinned when I saw him. That smile went ear-to-ear. You'd think he'd won the lottery with a smile like that. He didn't gloat though, a man like Bob Bage will never gloat. In fact, I'd be surprised if he ever insinuated a gloat. He wasn't arrogant, and he wasn't phony. Bob Bage was a man as gentle as the light of Venus, the first star to shine after sunset. Bob was as good as a man could get.

They told me he was the picture-perfect man for the obituary. Like I needed a reminder. You could tell just by looking at the man what a down-right goody two shoes he was. Buttons done up, one in each hole. His hair always brushed; moustache combed. And his shoes, oh, God, his shoes. You could eat your ration off of those shoes, he polished them every day. They shone like the Southern Cross they did. I can't help but wonder where his shoes are now. Are they sitting by his doorstep, having been mailed home after the battle? Empty and cold without use, but nevertheless spotless? Placed by the door too neatly, with not a lace out of place. Or perhaps they were in a box, shoved to the back of a shelf to collect dust until some years later a greasy little kid decides to go for a walk. I bet you they'd tie up the laces alright. The thought of it upsets me. Maybe he's still down there, wondering why it's so dark and dingy, trying to look for the stars without any success.

That day when they didn't announce his name in the survivors list, I'd thought I'd missed something. It's hard to believe a man like Bob Bage is gone, trust me on that if nothing else. I thought I must've been dreaming; Bob couldn't be gone. He wasn't done yet, not like all those other men. The Bob I knew was out there lecturing some innocent man about stars and constellations, going on expeditions and smoking a wooden pipe. The Bob I knew was walking around with his shoelaces untied and hiding the shaving cream because he refused to shave the beard, he worked so hard on. The Bob I knew wasn't lying under six feet of dirt in an Australian cemetery, alone and without a map. The Bob I knew hadn't been gunned down the moment he set foot, wounded and dead before he hit the ground. The Bob I knew wasn't some faceless name at a funeral service, wasn't "some guy" that you could cry a few tears for and then move on with your life, like he didn't matter. In the reality of it, thirty years or so from now, nearly nobody would remember him. Sure, they'd give their prayers and say their thanks, but they don't really care.

They didn't know the guy behind each gun.

They didn't know that Bob and I had to go back to the Antarctic to continue mapping the stars, mapping the tides, measuring magnetic fields, measuring our humanity against nature, to serve science and physics and serve the world to understand itself! They didn't! What a pity!

"So here I am, standing in a cemetery, wearing a jacket that's too thin and a hat that's too tight. On a Sunday morning where everything is too wet. All for you. In a world where the stars are still around, but you're not. We never thought you'd wind up down there. That's a nice headstone you've got, marble huh? Doesn't do you any good though.

'Bob Bage. Australian Soldier and Adventurer, 17th of April 1888 to the 7th of May 1915.'

I suppose I'm being childish about this, all sore that you're stuck down there, but I'm up here. I miss ya' alright? I didn't expect myself to care this much, but I do. I hope they know that. I hope *you* know that."

I huffed and fidgeted, something about cemeteries give me the shivers. That cold, damp feeling of "gone". I could practically feel my bones jittering.

"Christ... what can I say to you, Bob? I'm late and I know I am. I'm sorry, alright? Four years late, what a doozy... I sort of wish I hadn't shown up at all. I guess it never quite hit me hard enough. But I'm here now. Four years after you died, talking to a marble headstone that doesn't do you any justice, all alone in some random cemetery you never got to see. I guess I kinda hoped it was fake. The whole thing, you being dead and all y' know? I thought maybe I'd walk down to the shops one day, I'd be out of milk, and I'd see you. I'd see you standing in the frozen aisle, looking for milk too. Your beard would be back, and you be covering the sliding doors with smoke from your pipe. But I guess that's just plain dreamin'."

I didn't have anything else to say after that, not anything important really. I looked at the flowers I brought. I bought them at a little crumbling floral shop, just down the road. I thought Bob would've liked them. I leant down and put them on the soil, my hat nearly falling off. Standing up I readjusted myself, took a minute to bring myself together. I wouldn't cry, couldn't bring myself to do it. I stared down at him as I heard the noise of a shooting star in the sky. Is that perhaps the star that guided us to the South Pole? Is it saying "Goodbye"? Is it saying, "I am here to cry for Bob"? Heavy rain followed the shooting star. I watched as the soil turned even damper than before, watched as the rain streaked down the headstone. Watched how the water clotted on the blue petals of the forget-me-nots. No, it wasn't me crying, it was just the rain. Yes, that was it, nothing but rain.

"Goodbye, Bob."

I left.

I visited his mother at their Chemist store in St Kilda.

When she saw me, she put on her best dress and best hat. She asked me to go with her. We walked arm-in-arm to the University of Melbourne from where Bob had graduated in Civil Engineering.

Mrs Bage donated one thousand pounds for an Engineering scholarship to the value of forty pounds per annum. That's the kind of family they were. Givers for humanity.

Casey Ennis

The tragedy of death

Oh how Wonderful:
"What a wonderful way to die",
is a wonderfully wretched lie,
told to mothers, told to wives,
"How heroically they gave up their lives"?

"Your son was loved, he was brave,
he floats now in an ocean grave",
it's an ugly thing but still the truth;
"Your son has died a heroic youth".

"Poor ol' boy, the lad was shot"
his body left behind to rot,
"Poor ol' boy, between the eyes..."
never listen to the letter's lies,

A foreign land, a foreign grave,
"He's the one we couldn't save"
a thousand crosses, a thousand more,
made up of wood left by the shore,

"Paper, paper! Look what fame"
all go by "Unknown Name",
headlines say the "Country's Best",
but they all lay among the rest.

"Was he fearless? Tell me please!"
Colonels fear the mother's pleads,
No good response, they hang their head,
"He set off a mine on his first step".

Papers picture heroic boys,
Poets say the general's toys,
a telegram's the last goodbye,
there is no wonderful way to die.

Casey Ennis

1940 – Second Generation of ANZACs

Ode to Felix Craig Lovell[4] fallen in Farsala

Friday morning, 18 April 1941, the skies looked into your
bright blue eyes, Felix!
As you lowered your line of vision from the skies,
another pair of hazy hazel eyes was looking straight into
your own eyes,
with wide welcoming smiles.
A young Greek woman appeared in your face, out of nowhere!
You felt a little embarrassed how a young lass
outmanoeuvred your military tracking skills!
But then you thought, hey, these mountain girls
are better skilled in climbing hills,
than a Chartered Accountant from the plain fields of Ararat.
And then,
you were even more embarrassed as the youngster, leaned,
held your hands and kissed them softly, before placing her
offerings in front of you.

---

4 Felix Lovell Craig, born on 6 September 1914, was an Accountant and Auditor, from Ararat, Victoria. Private Craig enlisted at the South Melbourne Recruitment Centre on 23rd October 1939. He served as a driver in the Australian Army Service Corps, 16 Brigade Composite Company. Felix was killed in action in Farsala, Greece on 18 April 1941, age 26 years. He was buried at Phaleron War Cemetery, Greece. Private Felix Craig engaged the German dive-bomber planes with a machine gun and, while making himself a target until he was killed, he allowed other trucks with Australian soldiers to escape.

Freshly made white cheese, bright black olives, red ripe tomatoes, steaming hot bread!

You flashed a little, but you understood, you felt the meaning of the gesture.
It was to say thank you for coming to fight for freedom,
in the land of the Olympian Gods and of Democracy!

You looked behind the girl with more surprise in your eyes!
Walking up the mountain, the sound of many clogs almost betraying your position,
more Greek maidens, bringing food, and smiles and human feelings,
to all the ANZAC troops!

You were overtaken by a feeling of humanity, admiration, resilience,
as these Greek maidens, who could not afford to buy shoes,
were willing to share their scarce food with all your mates and comrades.
For them, the war was in its seventh month,
for you it was just beginning.
For all of you, the threat of barbarity was worth fighting for.

Most of the men in Farsala had been fighting the Italian armies for six months,
and most of the women in Farsala
were getting ready to join the men fight the German advance,
when they saw you, Felix, driving a truck full of young ANZAC soldiers.

Their first thought was food! Food and sustenance for these young men,
Who came on a boat, from the other side of the globe,
to help the Greek people defend Europe from fascism and barbarity.

Felix, the sudden presence, and the generosity of those young women,
gave you strength, gave you a belief in the fight of good over evil.

As the young ANZAC men disembarked from your truck,
to share food, hospitality, and the human touch,
the evil planes appeared and dived for their first attack.

The sound of the falling missiles brought no fear to your happy blue eyes
as they had just witnessed the reasons we love life,
humanity, respect, kindness, and love,
brought about by the appearance of the maidens and their touch.

We know Felix!
No fear, no sound would weaken your ANZAC spirit!
It was then you remembered your uncles Harold[5] and Fred[6],
11th Light Horse Regiment, killed in Palestine, in 1918,
and your cousin Archie[7], killed in Belgium in 1917.

---

5 Harold Hamilton Harlow, 11th Australian Light Horse Regiment, killed in Palestine, 1 May 1918.

6 Frederick Garnet Farlow, 11th Australian Light Horse Regiment, killed in Palestine, 25 September 1918.

7 Archibald Reginald Craig, 51st Australian Infantry Battalion, killed in Belgium, 13 October 1917.

Your family's legacy is never forgotten.
Your family's bravery is never downtrodden.

You called to the girls to hide in the hills as they knew best,
you called the other drivers to save the rest,
as you decided you will stand your spot,
as you climbed your machine gun, to shoot and be shot.

Felix, you fired away your brave song,
Felix, you fired away your brave soul,
you fired away your youth,
to save the young men around you!
Felix, you fired away your precious life, your precious blood,
to save the precious flowers of Greece and of Farsala!

The raid has ended, and the planes are gone.
Felix is now a fallen hero, and everyone will remember his song.

Liberty, legacy, love, and duty!
This is the story of the ANZAC family,
fulfilling their duty of honour against calamity.

John Milides

1956 — 16th Olympiad in Melbourne

In 1956, the 16th Olympic Games were held in Melbourne. Australians celebrated the performance of three wonderful athletes. Dawn Fraser won gold medals in the 100m freestyle and 4x100m freestyle and a silver in the 400m freestyle. Betty Cuthbert, also known as the 'golden girl' of the 1956 Melbourne Olympics, won gold in the 100 metres, 200 metres and 4 x 100 metres relay. Her 100-metre time of 11.4 seconds set an Olympic record. If Cuthbert was the golden girl, then swimmer Murray Rose was the golden boy. Rose was hailed a national hero after winning three gold medals and becoming the youngest Olympian to have ever been awarded three gold medals within a single Olympic Games. He won in the 400 metre and 500 metre freestyle events as well as the 4 x 200 metre freestyle relay.

Ron Clarke carries the flame around the arena during the opening ceremony at the Melbourne 1956 Olympics. Credit: Fairfax archives

Autograph hunters at the athletes' village, Heidelberg, 1956. Credit: © Herald & Weekly Times

Olympia's arrival in Melbourne in 1956

They do not come to Melbourne too often
but when they do
the athletes realise that
the gumtrees
are more beautiful than they imagined
the koalas
are friendlier than they expected
and this city is more peaceful
than the napping wombats in their burrows.

The Olympic flame sailed from the Aegean Sea
to the other side of the world.

Holding the precious flame
Olympia said good morning to the Indian Ocean,
greeted the Pacific Ocean with kindness
and thanked the Southern Ocean for the hospitality.

What a pleasant surprise when she entered the port of Melbourne!

This city on the South of the globe
thousands of miles distant
from the mythical land of the Gods,
was not much different from Olympia,
the birthplace of the Olympic Games!

Melbourne!
A city of athletes and sportsmen!
A city of kind men and women
who love to live and play
in round and oval green fields,
under the shade of the gum trees,
under the hot Australian sun.

The athletes gathered, at the docks of Port Melbourne,
waving, calling, "Yeia sou" Olympia,
welcome Olympia!
Thank you for bringing us
the flame of Peace,
the flame of kind sportsmanship,
the light of brotherhood,
the vision for a healthy body and a healthy mind!

Olympia was moved to tears by the welcome!

The flame kindly reminded her to stand tall and proud,
worried that overcome by emotion
Olympia could drop the torch into the sea
and then how do we begin these games,
that we waited for so many years

to cross three Oceans and arrive
to the first Southern Hemisphere Games,
in the land of the Southern Cross!

Olympia could not imagine
the warm welcome!
And then another surprise.

In the Antipodes,
Melbourne
counted a lot more sports men and women
than Olympia!
But she was not envious,
she was not unhappy.
she gave birth to the Olympic Games
to plant the seed of kind and pure athleticism
to nurture the body and nurture the mind
of all people,
men and women!

And then the revelation of sportsmanship in Melbourne!

Olympia witnessed Dawn Fraser and Murray Rose
swimming faster than the dolphins of the Aegean Sea!
Betty Cuthbert, the Golden Girl,
speedier than the blessed deer
of the Goddess Artemis!

As Betty won the 100-meter sprint
and then unbelievably the 200-meter sprint,

Olympia could not hold back.
She ran to crown the Golden Betty
with an olive wreath,
she brought with her
from the sacred sanctuary of Zeus,
Protector and Honoured God of the Olympic Games.

But Betty kept running as she had the hardest challenge yet,
to win the 400-metre relay.
Olympia could not believe her eyes and her senses on that day!
It was as though Aeolus, the keeper God of the Winds,
came secretly on Olympia's boat from Greece
and sided with Betty Cuthbert!
How else could Olympia explain this.
This girl had winds in her stride!
This girl was the daughter of the wind and the earth!
Betty won the day, Betty won the relay, Betty won the world!

Olympia made her decision
with Aeolus and Zeus' blessing.
She wanted to take the Golden Girl
with her, back to the glorious city of Olympia,
the mother of the Olympic Spirit.

She put her plan to action.
Betty, she said, the Gods are with you,
this was obvious in the Games!
And they have a plan for you, my golden girl!
The Gods are asking that you come and live in Greece,
they want to make you the Queen of the Olympic Games!

They offer you this glory
and they offered this to no-one
before you!
And Betty simply said with a sweet smile,
"But I love Melbourne by a mile."
A simple, humble answer with no arrogance.
Betty loved to run for her city,
not for extravagance!

The athletes do not come to Melbourne too often,
but when they come
they realise the athletes in this city
are taller than the gum trees,
friendlier than the koalas,
kinder than the timid wombats.

The athletes of Melbourne
are faster than the dolphins of the Aegean,
speedier than the sacred deer of Artemis,
and they love their city,
as dolphins love the water,
as athletes love to conquer!

John Milides

100m race, left-right: Isabelle Daniels, Giuseppina Leone, Betty Cuthbert 1st, Marlene Mathews 3rd, Heather Armitage, Christa Stubnick 2nd.

Olympia travels South

Olympia came to our land in 1956
in Melbourne where we competed
men and women from across the world
meeting with joy in the friendly games
holding our banner in the land down under
in the land of the South
under our hot Australian sun
the land of koala and the eucalyptus gum.

Our national heroes Rose and Betty,
champions in the Melbourne 1956 Olympic Games,
our heroes, the stars of their games,
our Rose claimed gold
at our games in the South,
at 17 years in 1956,
Rose's gold in the 400 and 1500 m freestyle,
while his team broke the world record of the 4 by 200 m relay.

It was like he became a fish that served us all the winning dish,
one gold with his team and two more by himself,
the Seaweed streak he was called,
nothing to do with his speed,
it was from what he ate, his seaweed diet,

he was strict and it paid off,
he became a national treasure.
Betty Cuthbert,
our golden girl at 18.
Gold in the sprints of 100m and 200m and 400m relay,
our golden girl, our Betty.
It seemed as if the air was her friend,
for they became one.
That year,
for everyone,
for all the others in that race, gold was gone.
She cut the line through the air that day,
nothing holding her back,
as if no drag existed around her,
it looked as if the air pulled her forward,
gaining her victories;
she was our girl who gave us winnings in three races that day.
One with her team,
the other two, herself,
but I'd say,
how she kept winning was if the air would say,
this girl is fast, so now I say,
I will help her win something today,
hard work pays off sometimes,
but not always,
but for Betty it worked that day,
our Rose, our Seaweed treasure,
our Betty, our golden girl.
They two brought us treasure in 1956,
6 gold of our 13 we won which brought us glory.

Olympia came to our land that year,
she was pleased for the things we won,
for she blessed us with glory
underneath our burning Australia sun.

Divinia Kihara

Betty Cuthbert wins the women's 4x100m final at the 1956 Melbourne Olympics, beating Great Britain's Heather Armitage (left). Image credit: Popperfoto/Getty

Murray Rose

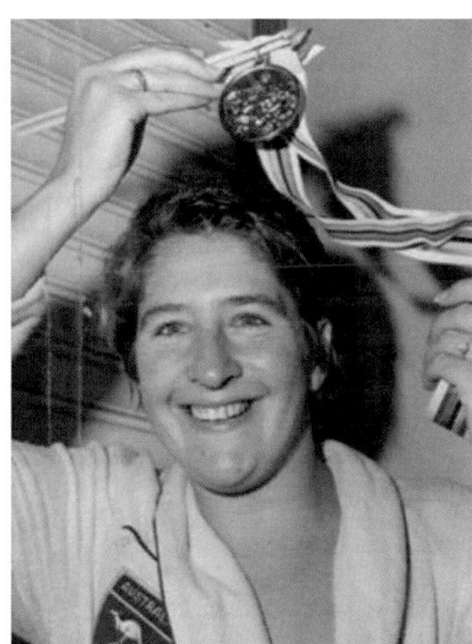

Dawn Frazer

1950 – 1970 — Melbourne Multicultural City

"Between 1945 and 1965, two million immigrants arrived in Australia. The decision by the Australian Government to open up the nation in this way was based on the notion of 'populate or perish' that emerged in the wake of the Second World War. Among the new immigrants were the first government-sanctioned non-British migrants. This massive influx of people transformed Australian society." National Museum Australia

"Even in the darkest days of the awful conflict of the Pacific war, the Curtin Government gave much thought to population building. I remember Mr. Curtin telling Cabinet in 1944 that at war's end there would have to be a Ministry for Immigration. He said we must have more people to develop and defend Australia."

Arthur Calwell, Australia's first Minister for Immigration, July 1945.

Dutch migrants on board the ship SIBAJAK arrive in Port Melbourne, 1954

Migration Story

I was forlorn and alone in a sea of nameless faces.
The Goya[8] was afar already.
Rocking slightly from left to right,
with the force of the waves, dragging it along.
Dry land of greys and reds,
rough sands and my barefoot standing,
faces of pale, ghostly looking,
why wasn't there a smile?
They stare; gazing as if I were unearthly.
I held out my hand,
they did not look at it, nor did they shake it.
With faces of gradual dismay.
I turned back to the sea.
The Goya was gone now.
I looked at the children,
running along the shore,
feeling the cool waters,
and wearing only shorts or loose dresses
made from old cloth.

---

8 **MS *Goya***: a Norwegian ship that carried hundreds of Eastern European refugees to Australia and New Zealand in 1951.

I got my first job.
A builder.
We had a boss of vulgarity,
an insult a day, from him.
Racist was he, bringing me injustice and worry.
For words are the weapons with which we wound.
What coin shall pay the debt of mine?
Whilst I toil, I save not a penny?

The cost of bills was towering,
though I was hard at labour,
I did not receive the pay for my pain.

I was lost in unmeaningful conversation.
I tried to take in every word,
oh, how difficult when one has not a hint of a language.
I didn't mean to not say hello.
I didn't mean to not respond.

When I could not afford the rest,
I lived off the papaya tree by the small opening in the ground.
They called it a lake.
Children enjoyed sitting there,
when their father toiled through the day,
and their Mother at home,
cooking and cleaning.
Shaking the tree,
few fruits falling into my hands.
One for each child and one for myself.
We would sit by that lake,

under shelter of the papaya tree.
After work, later into the afternoon.
The children were different from the other adults.
They listened to my stories,
and laughed at my jokes,
and awaited my coming after my 8-hour working day.
Melbourne mother of pain
and mother of migrants
I gave you my life.

Larissa Blazevski

Imagine Melbourne in the future I imagine in Melbourne

Melbourne,
a city, nothing more,
my wish, my dream, my hope,
is, one day this definition will change,

I dream of a city that is not yours, but ours,
and theirs, and his, and hers, your neighbour's,
of empty pavements and government steps,
for there is no need to walk along them,

Of soft mellow voices, like a mother's to her child,
of quiet reminiscence, that of which you so tenderly recall,
of gentle arguments, of solitary disputes,
for there is no need to shout once more,

Deprived of grins — not even the cats should wear one,
nor should one feel the need to smirk,
with less smiles filled with clenched teeth,
for *real* ones could never be so heartlessly refuse.

I detest the thought of a thoughtless future,
of the sombre predictions that lack children's sparkling eyes,
that dare confuse nightmare with reality,
and protest that such accusations could never be true.

Argue with me, bicker for the sake of bickering, but I'm stone,
and stone cannot be convinced,
not for anything in the world, not in the past or present,
predict doomsday, and I argue in response.

You may very well be right, I digress, but do not agree,
it doesn't settle with me well, their prophecies,
but surely, you must confess,
that we may never change,
while soft mellow voices are quashed by the megaphone,
while empty streets fill with signs, fill with shouting and rage,
and congressmen wear their smiles like suits.
Is it not nice to hope?

Casey Ennis

How I would like the future of Melbourne

I would like to see Melbourne a clean and respectful city.
I hope to see this city with little to no litter,
a place where all residents are mindful and kind,
a place where the future generations to come
can live in harmony and peace
without the fear of environmental change,
being harassed or ridiculed for who they are.
Although we still have a long way to go,
I believe that this will be possible soon
if we all work together,
starting with baby steps
and gradually getting them bigger and bigger
until we have reached our end goal.
That is the Melbourne I wish to see in the future.

Sandra Panamthathu

Melbourne dream

I dream of my Melbourne to be a green haven of voices
from flocks of birds playing in kindergartens with children
from swimming pools full of dancing water lilies
from parents singing to the tunes of the birds.

I dream of my city to be a forest of friendly houses
with sunlight shining from inside their halls,
out into the new cobblestoned streets
where the milkman would be greeted with warm hearts
and the stone builder would be loved by the smiling moon
and the mothers would feed the beaming moon with honey,
bearing blossoming buds in their velvet clean hands.

I dream of my city floating on a pond of waterlilies
and young parents pushing their colourful infants in green carriages
walking on the green and gold mountains
planting seeds of justice and sustenance.

I dream with eyes wide open
seeing
the fisherman offering poetry to the teacher
the farmer offering wheat to the worker
the doctor offering doves to the scientist

and the next generation of kinder children is born
with justice and doves and bread and fish floating
in the hospital pool
and the newborn babies are named
by the poets of love,
as stalls of freshly baked bread, pure milk, and pure honey,
appear on the banks of a crystal blue river named Yarra,
while a new conscience has cleaned the climate
and a new unpolluting sustenance is developed in Melbourne
for all eternity and all mankind.

My Melbourne will have the youth of a new moon,
the mind of a new Spring season,
the voice of the clear snow in the coming winter,
the future of beautifully fresh ocean winds,
the coming of crystal-clear rains,
the birth of new humming bees,
the birth of a new humanity,
desired, defined, and advanced
by the new young generations of Melbourne.

John Milides